The Emergent Workplace

Understanding and Creating Adaptive Workplaces

The Emergent Workplace
Paul Heath and Clark Sept

Copy editor: June Langhoff

Cover Image Melinda K. Hall, "Chair No. 7", 2002 (used with permission of the artist)

Published in the United States by Business Place Strategies, Inc.

ISBN 978-0-9896985-0-4

About the Authors

*Originality is something that is easily exaggerated,
especially by authors contemplating their own work.*

John Kenneth Galbraith

Paul Heath is an accomplished strategic planning professional, recognized in the facility and workplace consulting arena nationwide as a leading expert in developing business-based workplace strategies and implementation. Paul has a B. Arch from Rensselaer Polytechnic Institute and an MA in Architecture and Urban Planning from UCLA.

Clark Sept has a national reputation as a leader in the development of workplace strategies and workplace change management in both private and public sectors. Clark has a BA Architecture from UC Berkeley, and an MBA from St. Mary's College of California.

Foreword

Forward, I pray, since we have come so far, and be it moon, or sun, or what you please. An if you please to call it a rush-candle, henceforth I vow it shall be so for me.

William Shakespeare

This thing called "workplace" is really rather ambiguous. Time was the workplace was a pretty uniform physical construct; but today the places people work are as varied as the people themselves.

I've known Paul and Clark professionally for many years, over which time I've learned first-hand how they approach their work. Theirs is a particular bias, explicitly focused on the people who occupy the workplace. They fully understand the nature of place, bringing to their clients a deep, industry-leading level of understanding of how places impact the people who use them for their work.

The Emergent Workplace is not a how-to book for workplace strategists. Instead, it makes known the essential principles of applying a strategic approach to the place where people work, which is constantly changing ("emergent"). They rightly assert that the vast majority of traditional workplaces are inadequate for supporting work today since those places are the product of decades-old thinking. They often refer to "rear view mirror" planning – basing future decisions on past truths. The problem with this approach to the workplace is that inevitably the future of work has much less to do with legacy ways of working than most people either realize or are willing to admit.

The world of work is changing at a mighty pace. We see headlines daily that refer to new products being obsolete before they hit the stores. The Emergent Workplace is about embracing the inevitability and ambiguity of the future, and learning from it. What the authors apply to this task is "uncommon sense", based on their decades of practical experience. Listen to their down-to-earth advice – it will guide you to your future workplace.

September, 2013 - San Jose, California

Don Doyle

In his role as Senior Manager of Acquisition Integration at Cisco Systems (and formerly as a workplace strategist at Cisco), Don is keenly aware of the impact of the workplace on high-performing, innovative organizations worldwide.

The Emergent Workplace

Table of Contents

Preface

"These (Intel, Microsoft, Google) and other tech
companies are scrambling to reinvent their business
models now that the old model — a stationary customer
sitting at a stationary desk — no longer applies."[1]

New York Times October 23, 2012

Today's workplace is not just not keeping up with businesses, and their need to compete, it's holding back companies and organizations reliant on knowledge workers to stay ahead. Falling behind in any competitive arena is a bad thing. Technologies and demographics have now changed dramatically enough that old workplace models no longer fit personal demands and business needs. The tech companies started the process. Now they are seeing the consequences in their own business models. They are no longer able to depend on users in fixed settings or comparable technology environments. Mobility and mash-ups are driving work. The need

---

1   Miller, Claire Cain and Somini Sengupta; "In Mobile World, Tech Giants Struggle to Get Up to Speed"; New York Times; October 23, 2012.

for multiple, redundant and morphing social, physical and technological networks is clear. Relationships and processes are rapidly evolving…workspace is not keeping up, at least not yet.

Who should care? Anyone who works in or runs a business should care because the old workplace does not foster new work. Evolutionary success in organizations makes businesses more successful. In our experience, people and culture are central to that evolutionary success – people drive change that is necessary for adaptation. The emergent workplace is complex, but at its core it is about people and their community and creating support for successful evolution and change.

Creating the new workplace demands a new way of looking at the world. We have found through our work that the most responsive workplace is one that emerges from well-structured interactions and observations that establish and understand future work and cultural characteristics. The emergent workplace is about the future. Finding it requires examination and conjecture about future patterns and relationships, not careful examination of the world of the past.

Having observed that the workplace is changing in some radical ways, we also want to note that it is not changing across the board. Nor should it. Not all business demands or organizational/cultural characteristics are amenable to, or will derive benefit from, the emergent workplace. For these organizations business as usual works just fine.

We find it a fascinating time to be engaged in creating workplaces for knowledge work that can respond to spontaneous changes in work and work culture. We think that now is the time for businesses to be looking at their workplace from a new perspective that opens opportunity and engages people in molding the future. Our perspective is based on reflections on our experience in workplace strategy, planning and change management over the past twenty-five years.

We will use the experiences of two of our Business Place Strategies, Inc. clients, Cisco Systems and the General Services Administration Mid-Atlantic Region, as examples to illustrate the nature of the emergent workplace and specific ideas and approaches. They represent different states of development of their emergent workplaces.

In 2003 Cisco Systems initiated a pilot to test a completely new direction for their workplace. Underlying the pilot was a test of Cisco's own mobile technologies to support a completely unassigned workspace environment. With BPS' support, the pilot was quickly followed by a proof of concept, which then proceeded to a multiple phased roll-out. Today their workplace program is called the Cisco Connected Workplace. Although it was not the original goal, Cisco's workplace approach is an excellent example of the emergent workplace.

In 2010 the General Services Administration (GSA) Mid-Atlantic Region (3) undertook a pilot to test the applicability of mobile work in their organizations (both the Public Building Service and Federal Acquisition Services). The pilot was well structured and supported both by leadership commitment and with adequate investments. Findings from the pilot were significant in that the mobile work approach provided important opportunities for most of the participants to modify their work practices in valuable ways without disturbing the work of the organizations as a whole. For our purposes, the pilot clearly opened the door to emergent work practices and behaviors.

CHAPTER ONE

The Emergent Workplace

P rofessional understanding of the workplace has changed significantly over the last twenty years. The traditional singular focus on workspace has been supplanted by a view that recognizes the inherent nature of work as best described by a larger more complex environment. This growth in the workplace planning field has recently led to the design of workplace environments that are characterized by their broad response to business, organizational, cultural, and technological needs and demands. It is an important change because it provides a richer environment for business and work practices to grow and adapt with greater speed and focus.

Today the workplace is universally thought of as an environment as a system that is defined and created by a range of contextual components. We find that models are important for the clarity that they can provide to both to us as practitioners and to our clients. There are a number of models that describe the evolving workplace as a system. We use a model that identifies seven major environmental components:

1. Employees – Our model focuses on the subjective development of the workplace and so people (employees) are central to that environment.

2. Organization – Business organization defines the structure of the workplace environment. It has both implicit and tacit qualities. It is also the place where visions and goals originate.

3. Work process – All work has underlying processes. Some are very strict and rigid while others are very loose and driven by product/end result. But processes underlie all work and help define significant characteristics of the workplace.

4. Culture – Culture is the underlying set of norms and behaviors that are the "glue" that holds an organization together.

5. Physical & technology space – All work happens within a set of physical and technology spaces. In many respects they are "pathways" that facilitate/support business interactions and processes.

6. Policies – Policies are a form of "governance" within the workplace providing both structure and expectations from many perspectives.

7. Support systems – Within those other components there are various support systems to also help support work; e.g. facilities, HR, etc.

The key to all workplace models is that they describe the workplace as a system of interrelated components. The interaction of these components defines the environment that is specific to each business or organization. From the inside view, that environment describes the employee experience; the outside view is what we often think of as the customer experience, or "the brand". Most importantly, changes in the realm of any of the components necessarily impacts the other components, and therefore employee experience and how each employee will behave in that environment. Although the seven components define every organization, each organization represents a truly unique context. It is a context that changes over time in response to changes in the seven components. We will look at the value and importance of the changing nature of the workplace environment further on.

Figure 1. Workplace Dimensions

THE TRADITIONAL WORKPLACE REVISITED

Workplace thinking has traditionally focused on the spatial component with an almost exclusionary emphasis on physical planning and design – the physical workspace itself. Architectural and interiors programming methods have matured over time to identify specific work needs defined in enough detail to "define the design problem". Time motion studies became valuable in identifying how people spent their time. By the 1990s it became apparent that if we wanted to respond to the work of the businesses, analysis of work processes and work flow was the next step in refining business needs. This was followed closely by the use of utilization studies and social network analysis. All of these tools were important in that they provided greater clarity to the nature of the work, work tasks, use of space and social linkages as they currently existed. They provide a rationale for developing the structure – or logic – of novel, "alternative" workplace approaches. The assumptions built into this traditional approach to workplace planning are important in the way that they begin to define outcomes.

Traditional Assumption: Use patterns and expectations can be well defined.

A major assumption in traditional planning is that both need and use can be clearly defined at the outset. Defining use patterns and expectations can then be used as a programmatic foundation for establishing key components and features of a new and more targeted workplace. Use patterns also describe behaviors, which are ultimately variable, though not recognized as an important planning parameter until recently. There is an extraordinarily wide range of potential use pattern types often focused on time spent in an activity, including: at an assigned desk, on the phone, doing routine work, doing concentrated focused work, at on-site meetings, away from the office at meetings/client sites/travel/working at home, etc. The key is that patterns are considered to be well defined, stable, and therefore predictable.

Traditional Assumption: Good research approaches can define key workplace features.

The increasing sophistication of workplace analysis tools suggests that we can define the nature, characteristics, and key elements of a wide range of workplace components from work processes to task needs to interaction/communication patterns. The assumption is that the research can establish workplace features that can act as a core set of elements that define a new workplace. So-called "needs-based" planning has always contended with the central issue of filtering for bias. How do you discern true needs versus "wants" and subjective "padding" of requirements to provide room for future negotiating by stakeholders. The needs are considered "definitive" in that they describe needed resources in the future. These might include: individual workspace types, sizes and features; meeting resource types, sizes and distribution; technology features; policy approaches, prescriptions, proscriptions and supports; etc.

Traditional Assumption: The tools create "a business fit".

Today's research approaches largely focus on analyzing the work of the individuals and organization related to the business itself. The individual and organizational work practices are, of course, adapted over years in the past, but also represent the foundation for continuing adaptations to support the organization's future. The assumption then, is that they establish a sound basis for workplaces, and especially workspaces, that are designed to support overall business and business-related individual needs. Business fit applies to a number of characteristics: the way people interact, the types of tasks they do; the tools they use; institutional supports; among others.

Traditional Assumption: Adaptations can be episodic.

Overall, the assumption is that the traditional workplace, or at least the physical workspace, can be treated as static and that adaptations can be addressed episodically in an upgrade or refresh cycle. This is a result of the time and capital investments required for typical workspace retrofits. The impact is that over time many aspects of the workplace no longer are a good business fit.

Traditional Assumption: Understanding today is a suitable basis for understanding tomorrow.

Central to traditional workplace planning is that identifying current state provides adequate input to describing an appropriate future state. Bruce Race, a planning consultant with RACE-STUDIO, refers to this approach as "rear view mirror planning". A simple example is a contracting officer's need to have a printer scanner at "their" desk because they are required to use wet signatures even though central files are digital. A simple policy change allowing the use of digital signatures (now increasingly common) dramatically changes their work patterns and support needs. Designing from the "rear view" works only until that policy change occurs.

Thirty years ago those of us in the workplace planning arena were relatively comfortable that work practices would not change rapidly enough to worry about effectiveness over the long term. The dilemma is that is not true today. The rear view mirror has less and less relevance. The effort to describe current state in ever more refined detail has to be used with the understanding that business itself and individual and organizational practices are changing with ever greater speed. New workplace environments take months/years to fully implement. It makes current work practices increasingly less applicable at move-in than they were at the research stage, never mind in years to come.

Creating better long term fit to business needs requires a newer set of assumptions – even dynamic assumptions - about the workplace that can then be used to build on established workplace analysis approaches.

THE EMERGENT WORKPLACE

The key to finding a new set of assumptions that can respond to characteristics of today's workplace is to respond to and reflect the relatively rapid evolution of the seven components of the workplace described above. The pace and nature of change within these components is neither consistent from one to the other nor even consistent within a single component. The complexity that arises out of these differences makes it difficult to understand and predict the dynamics of today's evolving workplace. Emergence is a concept from other fields (philosophy, systems theory, science, and art) that we believe applies to the workplace today.

"Emergence is the way complex systems and patterns arise out of a multiplicity of relatively simple interactions."

Wikipedia

Descriptions of emergence as a concept vary slightly depending on the field in which it is being applied. However, there are important common underlying characteristics that we can apply to the workplace:

- Emergent behaviors appear when a number of individual agents operate in an environment, forming more complex behaviors as a collective. Behaviors emerge from intricate causal relations between the participants in varying forms and scales. The resulting emergent behaviors can be predictable, but tend to be unpredictable and unprecedented as the scale and nature of interactions grow and change.

- Emergent behavior is contrasted by the concept of deterministic behavior, which is reliant on predictive solutions that are based on past experience.

- Emergent behaviors are not a property or result of any single participant. Therefore, the resulting behaviors cannot be understood by looking at the behaviors/ properties of the individual participants. You can't easily predict what behaviors will emerge by knowing about the inputs to the interaction. It is also difficult and often impossible to look at the emergent behaviors and identify the behaviors of the original participants, i.e. you can't analyze backwards.

- Emergent behavior, particularly in the workplace, is difficult to predict in part because the number of variables and actors involved increase the number of interactions and combinations significantly. However, many interactions can just create "noise" without leading to new behaviors. At the same time, significant behaviors can arise out of limited but influential sets of interactions.

- Emergent practices can result from the introduction of new tools or settings that are integrated by individuals or groups in new ways. Outcomes are unpredictable in the same ways as emergent behaviors. Some emergent practices are simply new ways of doing the same thing while others open new more efficient processes and approaches.

- Emergence does not refer to, or imply, either complexity or simplicity. Emergent behaviors can be understood to be different from the behavioral environment in which they develop. In the workplace environment these behaviors are often seen to be more efficient and effective, but they also may just be different. Emergence is open to the recombinant impacts of changes. With the introduction of any new feature, the context of the environment is forever changed, even if that same feature is later removed. The removal of a feature

builds on the experience of having added that feature;
it cannot erase the experience.

Emergent behaviors can be seen to be an outcome of new and often rapidly varying inputs and interactions. Those inputs and interactions also generate emergent practices and patterns with similar characteristics to emergent behavior. Workplace practices and patterns are a reflection of both individual and group activities. Anecdotal evidence suggests that individuals will often generate unexpected work practices or develop workplace use patterns as a response to new tools or policies. Emergence is a significant factor in the workplace impacting behaviors, work practices and patterns of use.

The reality is that workplace behaviors, practices and patterns have always been changing and therefore impacting the nature and needs of the workplace environment. Our observation is that they are changing more rapidly and the nature of the inputs to that environment are more influential in causing emergent rather than predictive properties. Looking ahead to planning for the emergent workplace, we can identify some important characteristics of that emergent workplace.

Emergence can occur from simple physical changes. In Cisco's CCW post pilot phase, the space became much more open and transparent with low translucent panels and glass in all rooms. One staff member commented that he was constantly "interrupted" because he kept seeing people with whom he needed to speak. Despite being constantly interrupted, he admitted that he made more progress in less time because of the opportunistic interaction, and realized he was being more productive. The new space allowed new behaviors and patterns to emerge and settle in.

Emergence can also occur from simple changes in the use of resources or tools. One group in GSA's Region 3 went almost entirely mobile. They quickly discovered that if they used instant messaging as a group practice they could replace the expectation of "having access to people" based on where they were assigned to sit. They all thought this change in practice made their communications more immediate and consistent – a small emergent practice that had important work impacts.

Characteristic: Interactive use patterns can develop/change rapidly.

People are often quite responsive to new inputs, influences, tools or expectations. If it makes their work easier or more effective, people will quickly create or adopt new approaches to work. As work and the workplace has become more "open source" in nature, with increasing inputs from vastly disparate sources, the development of new or modified work patterns and practices has come faster and faster. This increase in inputs leads to more rapid development of emergent patterns and practices. New inputs cannot be turned off, *per se*, as new information keeps coming. There's a potential for too much information and the undermining effect this can have on decision-making. The truth is that a choice or decision must be made at some point to advance, regardless of the state of the completeness of the data inputs.

Characteristic: Research is foundational not predictive.

Workplace research, or analysis, as described above can have significant value in describing and understanding "current state" of the workplace as an interactive environment. It is very important to understand current state before venturing onto future state so that you know key features and attributes of your starting position. But current state is not often a good predictor of future state. Trends may be good indicators (e.g. moving to greater mobile work patterns), but the nature of emergent patterns and practices is that they are not a logical result of current workplace features.

Characteristic: Be adaptable to "business fit" over time.

In most all cases, goals today demand the workplace directly support business needs – "business fit". That is increasingly difficult, even over short periods of time, with the changes from emergent workplace elements. An emergent workplace will have characteristics and features that allow it to be more responsive to these changing elements. The more idiosyncratic the design or narrow the uses the harder it is for the workplace to adapt, such as specially sized meeting spaces, space use "assignments", and use-limiting management policies. It is not an easy task, but well worth undertaking. Decisions cannot be put off until such time as the business stops changing!

One of Cisco's managers tells a story that emphasizes the business fit possibilities and the need for continuous adaptation in an emergent workplace. The story comes out of immediate supply chain management needs as a result of the Japanese tsunami in 2011. He tells it best: "Today I spent at least three hours at a rolling whiteboard in my neighborhood. Being so open, some people saw me and team members huddled around it and stopped by to see hear the discussion and, as it turned out, their name was already on our whiteboard list of people with whom we needed to discuss this proposal. Knocked those discussions out right then and there. This would not have happened in our old work environment and the proposal vetting would have taken much longer. It seemed like >50% of the people we needed to talk with just happened to come by due to the open collaborative space. This open space truly is helping us be more effective during this Japan crisis. It is paying for itself more than you know right now."

Characteristic: Adaptations are continuous.

There are no more plateaus when it comes to adaptation in the workplace. In previous workplace planning models it was fairly assumed that adaptations or changes in work would be relatively sporadic and could be dealt with from a workspace perspective as a step function. Not today. Because use patterns are rapidly changing, adaptations are much more continuous. Emergence is a continuous function. It demands the workplace be adaptive.

Characteristic: Organization and culture are significant influences.

Organizations (relationships, management, structure, processes) have the greatest potential for continual integration of, and adaptation to, new and effective emergent behaviors/characteristics/structures. Unlike individuals, organizations can be restructured in response to business drivers, with the intention of greater outputs and performance. It might be said that deliberate change is necessarily part of the life of any successful organization. Organizational investment is in people (which appreciate), as opposed to capital investment in things (which depreciate). Behavioral adaptation (the people, not the organization) is not directly subject to budgets and accounting principles in the same way that space and technology are because it is qualitative (even abstract) whereas budgets and accounting are quantitative (even tangible). Culture

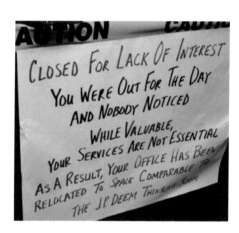

Culture will tell us how people interact with each other. It will tell us about how people feel about how they fit into an organization. Are they comfortable with joking with their supervisors? With each other?

adapts much more slowly as an outgrowth of the common desires of the people of an organization. However, it too is created out of the same interactions and relationships that lead to emergent behaviors and practices regardless the rate of change. While it changes more slowly, organization and culture is a rich environment for positive and effective ongoing adaptation.

Characteristic: Workplace is as much an idea as a physical place.

"I'm going to the office" used to be appropriate because it was a specific place we did our work. Today we are more often than not simply obliged to accomplish some piece of work, and place (i.e. the work venue) – as we have traditionally understood and assigned it – no longer matters as much for knowledge workers. Workspace is important because everyone has to sit somewhere, but business demands and inputs, the technology space, the organizational construct and the culture are increasingly the most demanding elements of the workplace.

WHAT MAKES EMERGENCE SO NOTICEABLE TODAY?

People have always been interacting as co-actors in the dynamics of the workplace. Why should emergent behaviors and practices be so much more noticeable and important today than they used to be? Many interactions do not create impacts that are noticeable, i.e. they are just work/organizational "noise". They are not interactions that create new behaviors or practices. "Workplace speed" has increased significantly – speed of information, speed of interaction, speed of decision-making, speed of introduction of new tools and techniques. Emergent behaviors and practices may simply be developing faster than they used to and therefore are more noticeable and impactful. Finally, and most important, there are inputs to work and the workplace that are forceful enough in their own right to precipitate emergent behaviors and practices. There are four significant workplace inputs impacting us today.

1. IP-Based Interactions – You can now engage in most elements of work with people anywhere in the world through IP (Internet protocol) based mechanisms. There are three important characteristics of this IP environment that feed emergent practices and behaviors.

First, technologies are extraordinarily flexible, diverse and powerful. The array of technologies that integrate data and communications in completely mobile form creates vast opportunity and demand for new forms of work practice. You can now communicate and interact through multiple devices, channels and locations at will, twenty-four hours a day (if you want to).

People are using their mobile tools in remarkable ways – phones for email, web interactions, creating WiFi hotspots, even for phone calls. One of GSA's Region 3 staff developed an "app" that could be used to check into a workspace on-the-fly.

Second, geography is significantly less relevant, in terms of work process and time. The transition from hard copy data to electronic data has reached an important level of maturity. Our observation is that the vast majority (but certainly not all – yet) of data and information is now dealt with electronically rather than in paper form. Most importantly, because of the breadth and strength of IP-based technologies you can now effectively work anywhere, and exchange that data with others at will. We no longer have to depend on being in a specific place to access data we are working with, i.e. getting our hands on some paper-based data. However, geography remains important from a culture perspective, particularly for the organization whose workforce is distributed across time zones and continents. That said, we pose the following question: is technology neutralizing cultural syntax as pertains to organizations? If so, what are the implications on the emergence of culture in organizations?

Third, it's still new. The most agile and mobile technologies are relatively new and just being applied in the workplace.

> The original iPhone is now obsolete, just six years after introduction.

There is no "this is the way we do it here" with respect to these new opportunities. So people are simply trying new things and sharing the ideas – new emerging practices and behaviors.

2. The Cloud – "The Cloud" is a more subtle, but very important addition to IP-based interactions and information. The IP basis separates us from geography. The Cloud takes access to that information outside of the constraints and limitations of traditional business firewalls and required direct network access. It is now possible to access pertinent information wherever and whenever you need with an Internet connection. We're discovering that people are extraordinarily creative in their use of the ability to access information when they are not "at their desk". In fact, many people no longer find the need for an assigned desk. They simply prefer to work wherever it is that suits their purposes the best. Assigning seats no longer makes sense – it is an increasingly obsolete management control rubric.

3. Distributed organizations – Business is no longer constrained to work on a centralized model. Geography is less relevant, so demands for centralizing an organization have lessened significantly because work can be done anywhere. Organizations are a manifestation of the joint efforts of those co-actors described earlier. The larger the organization, the more location and linkages between multiple locations become relevant to the ability and capacity of an organization to evolve and adapt in response to changes in the world. There are multiple drivers, but the end result is that many organizations have people in diverse locations all with the need to routinely interact with each other. Once you have people in multiple locations, the need to interact and share in work flow leads inevitably to emergent practices and behaviors simply by taking advantage of new opportunities. These tend to change both overall workplace and workspace practices and patterns. One of the very consistent patterns we observe is that managers experience pressure to manage more by outcomes than by task as organizations become increasingly distributed and mobile.

GSA Region 3's mobility pilot had one serendipitous and important support. Just prior to undertaking the pilot project, GSA rolled-out the Google Suite on a national basis. Working in the cloud allowed the Region 3 staff to work from anywhere they needed to without concern for access behind the organizational network firewall. One staff member described working on a document simultaneously with a co-worker to meet a critical and unexpected deadline – while on an airplane! A process made possible through the cloud (and Google's interactive suite of tools).

4. New expectations – The demand for tools, options and freedom to use them is significant. Common analysis suggests that it is the younger demographic that is driving these new expectations. Our experience is that there are plenty of people in all demographics that are using the new tools and resources to their benefit and therefore asking for more. Some of them have leverage or influence, so the demands and response will continue to feed the emergent environment.

THE EMERGENT WORKPLACE DILEMMA

Emergence occurs quickly. Workspace does not. That is the central emergent workplace dilemma. Workspace is expensive, it takes time to plan and build, and it is expected to last from 1.0 to 2.0 to 3.0 cycles, unfortunately often as long as fifteen years or more before the next refresh. Changes are happening at a much faster clip, and by definition emergent characteristics can't be predefined during planning. Decades ago we recognized that one approach to outdoor open space design is to establish the activity points and let the connecting paths emerge through use. You then formalized the paths and looked clever in understanding what the paths were. In workspace design it is not as easily done because of the nature of the variables and investments. Focusing design on activity points and allowing patterns of use and behavior to emerge is one approach that has been used in other design settings. It is an approach we will address later in Part 3, "Creating the Emergent Workplace. This is the core dilemma of designing the emergent workplace.

PROSPECTIVE RISK

The adaptive capacity of the conventional workplace, versus that of the emergent workplace focuses in part on an organization's posture towards risk. Several business risk issues relate to the formation of workplace strategy:

Risk Factor: Appetite for investing in the future.

What is the availability and disposition of the organization to invest in the future (monetary and political capital)? Long-term thinking and investing are not evenly distributed among businesses or organizations, or even across organizations within the same company or agency. Emergence can occur over the short term, but short term business thinking tends to limit the acceptance of change necessary for that emergence to occur. Prospective change is simply not high on the agenda in many cases.

Risk Factor: Business cycle time frames.

How is the relevant development time frame innate to the business itself, compared with the time required to adapt the workplace to meet the businesses' needs? Business cycles vary considerably as does their influence on work practices. Rapid cycles quickly outpace the ability of workplace supports (physical and technology space and even policies) to respond. It is an inherent tension with emergent practices behaviors and patterns.

Risk Factor: Change Sensitivity.

What is the capacity of the organization to adapt to change, and what time-frame applies to adapting to change? Some organizations are not well adapted to accepting change; they move more slowly in response to all types of internal and external influences. Some are simply averse to change both from an organizational and staff perspective. They tend to accept less risk in their evolution. Other organizations thrive on change because it matches with their business model and/or defines them culturally. They accept much higher levels of risk. The time frames for change will be significantly different depending on the inherent adaptation to change and the acceptable risk.

Risk Factor: Rate of change.

What is the relative rate of adoption of emergent work practices? This is a characteristic linked with the ones above. Emergence happens everywhere in the workplace, but our observation is that it happens more rapidly and with greater influence in organizations that move quicker, are accepting of change, and where individuals are free to develop their own effective approaches to work. It also happens more quickly where people communicate and interact frequently and consistently as we saw with the GSA Region 3 group described on page 18.

Based on important organizational and cultural characteristics as a communication tool with our clients, we have developed a model of adaptability "Organizational Adaptability Characteristics, (Figure 2.) on the following page.

Figure 2. Organizational Adaptability Characteristics

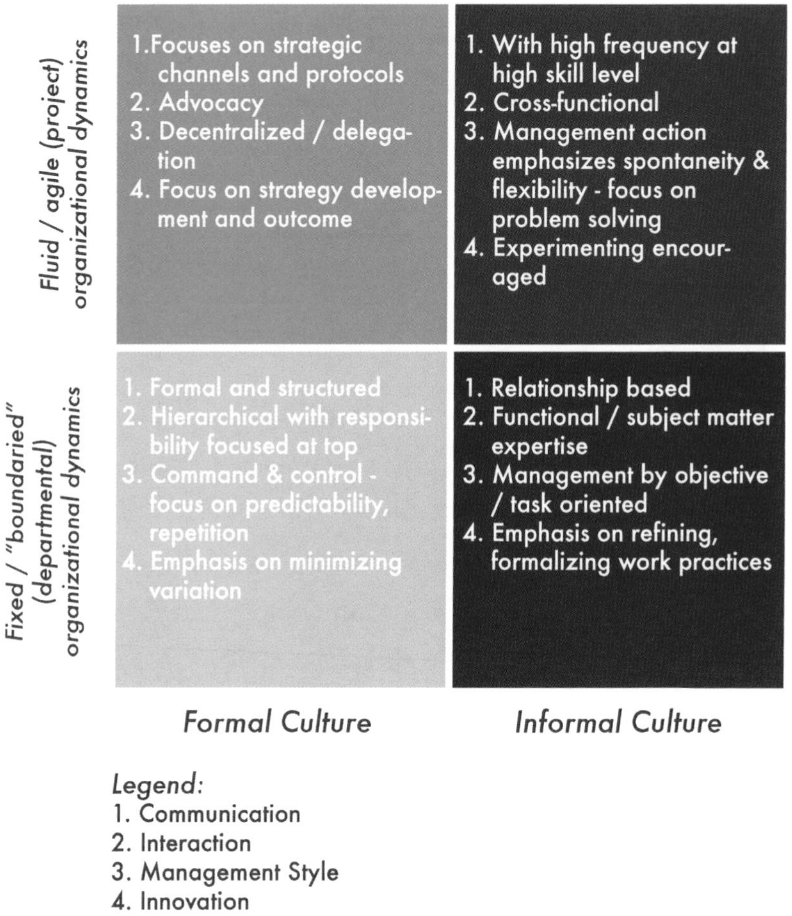

Fluid / agile (project) organizational dynamics

1. Focuses on strategic channels and protocols
2. Advocacy
3. Decentralized / delegation
4. Focus on strategy development and outcome

1. With high frequency at high skill level
2. Cross-functional
3. Management action emphasizes spontaneity & flexibility - focus on problem solving
4. Experimenting encouraged

Fixed / "boundaried" (departmental) organizational dynamics

1. Formal and structured
2. Hierarchical with responsibility focused at top
3. Command & control - focus on predictability, repetition
4. Emphasis on minimizing variation

1. Relationship based
2. Functional / subject matter expertise
3. Management by objective / task oriented
4. Emphasis on refining, formalizing work practices

Formal Culture   Informal Culture

Legend:
1. Communication
2. Interaction
3. Management Style
4. Innovation

CHAPTER TWO

Change is the Driver

O ur clients have had us spend a significant amount time over the last decade helping them with workplace "change management" to facilitate individual and organizational adaptation to new workplace environments. Change management is changing. It has, for a long time, been a dependent function that was important because someone (facilities or business leadership) decided it was important for some good reason to change the workspace environment. In a well-constructed process, work was done to facilitate adaptation to the new environment so that people and organizations could start quickly and take advantage of the opportunities inherent in the new environment. Today, change is no longer a dependent function. Change is now a key driver of business, work and the workplace.

> You cannot create and sustain an effective workplace if change is not understood as being an integral, formative element.

There are a variety of influences that are driving change beyond the four described above (IP-based interaction, the Cloud, distributed organizations, and new expectations). They all have important impacts that should be realized and addressed as part of the workplace, particularly as part of the emergent workplace. However, there are three areas of change that need particular attention to create and sustain an effective emergent workplace.

1. Individual Change – It all starts with the individual. We noted above that foundational workplace patterns and behaviors are the result of individual work and interactions. Change, and adaptation to change at the individual level, is the first of the significant components that supports the emergent workplace. People have an immense ability to adapt to new influences and needs within the workplace. Some people are strong change leaders and some are strong resistors. Yet overall, most people develop and share new and adaptive patterns, tools, ways of working and behaviors. Individuals are the key building block in the workplace environment. Focusing on active individual participation in change is the most critical attribute in any process that addresses developing and maintaining appropriate emergent workplaces.

GSA's Region 3 had a fully visible process, or at least we thought so. Everyone had the opportunity to participate in the pilot if they wanted to put their name in. The leadership provided regular communications regarding progress and expectations. The very active steering committee created avenues for people to find out what was happening and why. All staff had the opportunity to participate in surveys to evaluate the mobility approach and its impacts. Even with this broad communication, some people who were not participants in the pilot thought that they should have gotten all the information and training that

2. Organizational Change – Organizations hold the biggest potential to adapt to and take advantage of emergent patterns and behaviors. The key to organizational change and support lies in individuals recognizing the need and proactively moving to adapt – structure, relationships, policies, expectations, etc. Conscious organizational adaptation is a powerful tool since it can be done relatively quickly and without capital investment. It does, however, take investment in time and leadership commitment. Experience suggests it is not as easy as one might imagine. Organizational inertia is often difficult to overcome, including individual's investment in their understanding of what the organization is, how it works and what their role is in it. Turning inertia into momentum may not be easy (it may require investment of political capital), but it is a tremendous resource for the emergent workplace when an organization gets proper focus.

Figure 3. Individual-Organizational Relationships

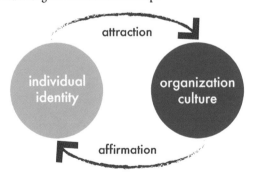

individual : member : organization

Individuals are attracted to organizations for their shared benefits, values and the opportunities they offer.

Organizations affirm (reward) the membership of individuals for what they contribute to the benefit of the group.

3. Workspace Change – Workspace change is actually more difficult than most people imagine, and certainly more difficult than change at the organizational level. The inherent time frames involved make changes to workspace difficult to adapt to short-term organizational change because of the lag in getting it planned and implemented. It also requires capital investment, which can be a serious impediment. So changes to the physical workspace happen infrequently. But it is a significant goal. The key is to find approaches that in fact can change and flex in a variety of ways – basic environments amenable to changes from a variety of activities. Workspace change is difficult, but not impossible, particularly when leveraging the opportunities created through people and organization.

TIPS FOR SUCCESSFUL WORKPLACE CHANGE

Change is most successful – and sustainable – when the conditions have been prepared to enable change to happen naturally. Conscious attention to change more effectively opens the door to and reinforces the impacts and benefits of emergent patterns and behaviors. The following tips on workplace change are specifically targeted to reinforce those impacts and benefits.

Make change visible.

Too often change is an invisible process of slow accretion, and when it happens behind closed doors, or "the curtain", it can prompt suspicion and cynicism. Change happens in spite of our best efforts to contain it. The more visible it becomes the more opportunities it can create. Visible change can be an important catalyst in that it opens people's thinking to new and potentially better ways of working. It creates opportunity simply because it opens doors in the way people think about what is possible. Our experience with workplace change shows that the more visible, open and transparent you make the change and process of change, the greater the individual and organizational benefits.

Change ... is sometimes scary!

Make change adaptive and relevant.

Too often we have seen workplace initiatives rolled out without warning or consideration for the potential impacts on organizations that are unprepared. From our experience we have learned well the lesson that prescriptive – cookie cutter – change programs too often fail. The failure is usually due to lack of relevance to the individuals impacted by the change. People are naturally adaptive, and will quickly develop clever workarounds to any change they feel is contrived and which impedes their ability to get their work done in the best way they know how. Though not necessarily subversive (although, sometimes...), this kind of response to change is a clear sign of inadequate preparation in advance of implementing change.

Focus on competencies.

Looked at overall, the workplace is background to the work itself. We don't have to focus on the workplace because we "know how it works" – we're competent in its use. Problems arise when the workplace changes and we can no longer assume that same level of competency. Changing any of the six elements of the workplace distracts us, and causes us to have to devote time, attention and energy focusing on using the environment rather than doing our work. The dilemma is that we fall to a different place in the "four stages of competency"[1]. As a theory about learning, it describes how we go from literally not-knowing to not having to think about it.

Four Stages of Competency – We'll use tying your shoes to illustrate the development of learning how.

1. Unconscious incompetence: the first stage is of unrecognized unmet needs. We don't even know what we don't know. As a baby I don't even know I'll have shoes never mind how to tie them.

---

1   Known as "Four Stages of Learning", it was developed at Gordon Training International in the 1970s and is often attributed to Abraham Maslow from the 1940s.

2. Conscious incompetence: in the second stage we recognize a need or desire, but we still do not have the skill to practice it. I now know I need to tie my shoes, but Mom or Dad still need to do it for me.

3. Conscious competence: in the third stage we are mastering the skill set but still have to consciously attend to it in practice. We all remember having to think "this one goes over, this one goes under, and I pull…"

4. Unconscious competence: the final stage is one where the skill has become innate so that we can do and attend to other activities and tasks at the same time. When is the last time you thought about tying your shoes?

The four stages of competency play a central role in workplace change management. In an ongoing state we are all unconsciously competent in our use and understanding of the workplace overall. We do our work based on our tacit skill at knowing what the workplace provides for us and to us both as opportunity and constraint.

Change something in that workplace environment and we become less competent – consciously competent or even consciously incompetent. It makes our work harder to accomplish. A key to managing that change is to mitigate the amount time we spend working on regaining our workplace competency.

Learn from change.

You cannot control change, so it is important to integrate it as part of the natural process of workplace development. Too often we focus on a project, facilitate adaptation and then move on to the next one. Rare is the organization that spends its resources (time, but also money) to consciously address and take advantage of the opportunities inherent in ongoing workplace pattern and behavioral change. As we said before, change is most successful – and sustainable – when the conditions have been prepared to enable change to happen naturally. Individuals and organizations can and will evolve and adapt to new influences. Active attention to those changes can continue to facilitate the growth of an effective emergent workplace.

Our experience with workplace change management at Cisco began in the mid-1990s working with their field sales office teams, helping them adapt to the concept of sharing desks. When we got involved in crafting a change management approach for what evolved into their Cisco Connected Workplace (CCW) program at their corporate headquarters campus, the feedback was strong and positive relating to the value of investing time in the change management activities related to the changing workplace. The approach has since the early days become embedded within the organization. Cisco has developed a formalized corporate change management approach, with change leaders in every business unit. The real payoff for them as been not just more successful adaptation to ever-changing contexts, but development of the ability to learn from the changes, and adapt their initiatives on an ongoing basis. Borne out across the various business units that have had the chance to update to the CCW model, is the consistent finding that communication and employee satisfaction levels tend to rise within the organization as a direct result of the transition experience.

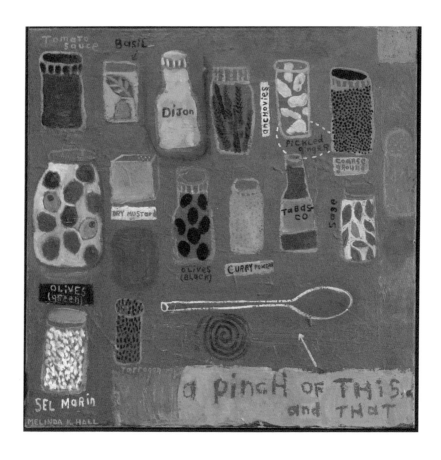

CHAPTER THREE

Creating the Emergent Workplace

We have seen many organizations struggle as they attempt to deliver a new type of workplace by applying their traditional processes. Creating an emergent workplace requires a more diverse perspective: from key workplace components, from a strategic perspective, from within an open process, all while speculating about the future. Process is an essential and formative aspect of creating the emergent workplace. The nature of the planning process, the discussions and understandings that develop, and the decisions about initial design features are all a foundation for the ongoing development of an emergent workplace. Envisioning, planning, designing and implementing the emergent workplace come about as a result of a process that is different than the traditional delivery process for conventional workplaces. Importantly, key stakeholders must pay attention and participate, because the emergent workplace develops over time not just when decisions are made related to planning and design. The emergent workplace can only be realized as a result of a highly integrated process (involving different timing and close coordination between groups that traditionally don't need to interact during the process), which is inherently more complicated than the process that results in "standard tenant improvement" space.

There are six considerations that are critical to emphasize, and balance, in creating the emergent workplace. The first three will be described further in this chapter, and the second three will be addressed in the following chapter, "Describing the Emergent Workplace."

The emergent workplace can look different from business to business depending on the details. However, there are some basic characteristics that you find in all emergent workplaces.

Openness – In all aspects of the workplace there are elements that are prescribed and others that are proscribed. In all cases there is "space" between them. This is where emergence has its greatest impact. The more open the "space", i.e. less is required or forbidden, the more emergent the workplace. For example: Work processes that tightly define methods are less open than those that focus on results only. Workspaces that are unassigned provide opportunities that assigned environments do not.

Flexibility – The six workplace components can be molded. The more elastic these components are, the greater the potential response to and support of emergent behaviors and practices. For example: Highly defined and bounded remote work policies (off-site, home, etc.) seriously limit opportunities and options with regard to development of new/more effective ways of working. In the physical and technology workspace, narrow single use resources are more limiting than flexible open-ended ones.

Choice – People are not limited to single sets of resources, settings, or approaches. For example: In the physical workspace people have multiple options on where to sit or work depending on need. The technology workspace is redundant or multi-channeled so that people can access what they need in a variety of ways.

---

1. ***Use a strategic perspective*** – Strategy, by its nature, focuses on the future. As a perspective, it assumes that the future will be different than we can make assumptions about or imagine today. That is the emergent workplace. There are many approaches to strategy; the key is to be future-focused and flexible in moving forward.

2. ***Leverage the workplace planning process*** – The characteristics, structure and pace of the process that is used to create the emergent workplace is central to its potential success. In this particular case, how you get there matters a lot because it is the process that generates meaning and investment.

3. ***Illuminate organization and culture*** – Organization and culture, the aggregate manifestation of individuals together, are the pulse and central nervous system of the active and inhabited workplace. They have to be a central focus of all workplace-creating processes.

4. ***Create physical workspace as a framework*** – The problem with emergence in the workplace is that we don't know what it looks like ahead of time. The goal for the physical workspace is to create a framework or structure amenable to new and different practices, patterns and behaviors that will emerge over time. Spaces that lack such qualities inhibit adaptive organizational dynamics.

5. ***Integrate the technology workspace*** – Technology is one of the key drivers of emergence in the workplace. It needs to be considered, discussed and included as a significant element of the emergent workplace.

6. ***Develop approaches to supporting the workplace*** – The emergent workplace's value is derived in part from the freedom that the occupants have to make decisions about how their workplace should be used. The nature of the support systems, from policies and procedures to physical and technological features, create significant opportunities or impacts on that freedom.

In principle, two threads drive the process of creating the emergent workplace. First, identifying emergent properties is at best "educated speculation". The process must establish an environment within which we can create and understand these speculations about potential future practices, patterns and behaviors. Knowing exactly what those characteristics will be is not possible; but, being open to future variability and opportunity is fundamental. Second, therefore, the emergent workplace – business, organization, culture, individuals, physical space and technology space – must be attentive and adaptable to the inevitably different workplace characteristics that will occur. The key is conscious attention, openness and adaptability.

THE STRATEGIC PERSPECTIVE

Strategy making or planning, what's the difference? In many respects the differences are subtle. Planning essentially focuses on creating a program of action that gets you to a specific "end" by creating a framework of tactics. Strategy focuses on overarching goals – or "ends" – that are established at a broader less specific level. You might have to undertake a number of plans, ways of moving forward, to meet strategic goals. A planning perspective is most effective when situations are well known and outcomes are knowable. A strategic perspective is needed when desired directions can be defined but mechanisms for getting there and specific outcomes inevitably will change during the course of action. A clear definition of strategy as it applies to creating the workplace might be borrowed from the biology arena:

> *"…an adaptation or complex of adaptations (as of behavior, metabolism, or structure) that serves or appears to serve an important function in achieving evolutionary success."*
>
> Webster's Dictionary

Evolutionary success in organizations is good business. What does it have to do with emergence and the workplace? Emergent practices, patterns and behaviors impact and change the workplace in ways that suggest a need for "adaptation or complex of adaptations". Since it is difficult to predict exact "endpoints" for a changing workplace, the approach to creating a new workplace should be strategic in nature. What is "strategic in nature"? There are five important characteristics of the strategic perspective:

1. ***Future oriented*** – Most critically, strategy focuses on what's coming, not on what's here now. The central issue for the emergent workplace is the future of the business. This means finding ways to speculate about what the future holds (see The Role of Process below) in terms of the nature of work, the tools that might be available, potential changes in processes and practices and growth and change within the organization and culture. The effort is based on today's workplace characteristics, but focused on what might emerge tomorrow.

2. **Adaptable** – Strategy comes from the military – *strategia,* from Greek – meaning generalship. Military plans designed to implement a strategy are a first move. A good strategy prepares you for counter-moves because the situation inevitably changes – from the outset. The same is true for workplace strategy. It has to be adaptable from all perspectives. In the aggregate, it recognizes and responds to the changing work needs of the business. The key is that those workplace needs will change and a strategy should build in mechanisms and approaches to adapt.

3. **Systemic** – The nature of strategy is to consider the interrelationship – linkages – among the parts. What directly impacts any element of a system will necessarily impact all the other elements of the system at least indirectly. Such impacts, which are often unintended consequences of a planned approach, need to be exposed and tested through the iterative process of developing and implementing a strategy.

4. **Opportunistic** – Strategy takes advantage of opportunities in the broad environment. We know now that changes to inputs, relationships, needs, etc. will occur – sometimes faster, sometimes slower. A key to successful strategy is embedding the ability to coherently respond. Some changes are clearly good opportunities to build on positive growth in the workplace environment. Some changes simply need to be ignored or, at times, modified to become something different. Part of what good strategy does is to make this recognition of opportunity a conscious activity that can leverage change to the benefit of the organization. Good strategies include all interrelated parts, and exclude considerations in the broader environment that will remain unaffected.

5. **_Directed_** – Good strategy is highly directed. It is focused on where you want/need to go. Goals matter. Tactics are responses to directional goals (or changes in direction) established by a strategy. For example, "share information" is a broad goal that has significant implications across the workplace elements – work process, physical space, technology space, cultural mores. As a goal it provides excellent guidance in creating a variety of supporting elements within a new workplace. The strategic goal would be "share information"; "build more conference rooms" would be a tactical response aimed at satisfying the strategic goal. There are lots of ways to promote sharing information, one of which may be to build more conference rooms. However, over time, even that level of goal may need to be modified, at least in the way it is understood. For example, even the goal, "share information efficiently" could be detrimental if it caused too much sharing. Those longer-term, somewhat subtle changes in direction are a natural part of the implementation of good strategy. In all cases, direction is needed at the strategic level.

Everything described above implies something different in the future. To get there you need to have direction, but you also need to know where you started – current state, position, opportunities and options. Looking back to the discussion about traditional workplace planning approaches and tools, it is clear now that good information about the current nature and characteristics of the workplace is an important baseline. As a starting point they are valuable, but they do not give you the basis for making decisions about potential future states and strategies to get there.

Figure 3. Workplace Characteristics - Conventional versus Emergent Workplaces

Conventional Workplace		Emergent Workplace
Extrapolation of proven planning algorithm based on set assumptions	Strategic discipline	Emphasis on future adaptability and opportunistic direction changes
Simple assignment of fixed resources to occupants based on headcount plus linear projections	Dominant characteristic	Fungibility of resources open to shared use reflecting present and emerging needs
Low due to inflexible "precinct boundaries" and rigid management controls over resources	Adaptive capacity	High given basic tenet of maximizing utility of resources through shared use
Sustains legacy organizational culture	Organizational culture impact	Disrupts legacy organizational culture – drives adaptive change

Traditional project delivery is typically a rote process. It is highly refined, based on years of doing it the same way, delivering the same solution each time in known ways. However, when the goal is to deliver and support a set of strategic solutions that are divergent from the usual approach, the traditional processes are inadequate. The emergent workplace recognizes connections between seemingly unrelated aspects of the workplace, thus requiring the process to be adaptive to the various and variable inputs. That said, misgivings crop up about undertaking an untested process to achieve unproven results. Often, the reluctance is related to not knowing whether the outcomes will prove effective. Another is the concern that it will take more time, and put the entire undertaking behind schedule. Then there's concern that doing it differently will cost more. We will seek to address these concerns in the following pages.

WORKPLACE STRATEGY PRINCIPLES

Strategy making is not a routine process done in a rote way, at least not successfully. It has to be done as a conscious activity specifically targeted to the situation at hand. We will cover the fundamentals of strategy making as a process in the next section. However, the underlying key is in the focus on the directions, needs, opportunities and issues of the specific business and workplace. The military analogy applies here as well, military strategies, in the end, are always focused on the specifics of the situation whether it is a battle or an overall campaign. Generalized strategies and approaches are understood and studied, but in the end strategies are very specific. The same is true for the workplace. General strategic approaches are well known in how to address a broad range of business and workplace goals. Good strategy has to be tailored and monitored to respond to emerging practices, patterns and behaviors. In the end, success depends on the engagement, commitments and resources specific to the business.

What would a workplace strategy address? An effective strategy accounts for the desired relationships among the related workplace parts. The categories that frame a workplace strategy are found in standard workplace planning practice today. The difference is that, in the case of the emergent workplace, we apply key strategy characteristics described above (future orientation, adaptability, opportunity, direction) to the interrelationships. The main categories, described below allow you to address all six components of the workplace.

Business goals.

Business goals are all about where the business is going which allows a workplace strategy to find a variety of ways to get there. These goals will inevitably focus on the workplace not just the workspace. Some will be actionable from all six of the workplace components while others will address only one or two. While there are some consistent themes out there today, the most critical element is to fashion goals that reflect the needs of each business / organization so that they establish direct relevance for all staff. Importantly, goals are very specific and often highly crafted by the business or organization. However, we have found over time that there are three big themes within which many goals and vision elements fall.

1. **Effectiveness** – It's about the operations of the business of the organization. These goals seek to increase "productivity" either directly or indirectly.

2. **Efficiency** – Focus is on effective and therefore efficient use of resources. In the end it is typically about saving money in some fashion.

3. **People / Culture / Image** – These represent the "soft" side of the organization, but cannot be discounted because they are critical to success. They tend to focus on staff, but can address culture and customers as well.

Each business must generate its own goals. This guarantees ownership of the goals and ensures that the goals apply directly to the actual work. Even though we identify general patterns of goals as described in the text, there can be significant variation given real investment by leadership in generating key goals. Two businesses describe the potential differences:

Business One – A software development business that was reconfiguring their workplace at a new location. The business leader was very clear and concise with his goals:

- "Wow"…a world-class facility.

- Create community and identity.

- Focus on collaboration.

- Create transparency.

- Attract people to the office.

- Efficient space utilization.

- Leverage furniture guidelines.

Business Two – A Federal Agency with a centralized campus that required a new workplace strategy to deal with growth and other real estate demands. The leadership team spent significant time crafting a set of thirteen goals that addressed the broadest understanding of the workplace:

To provide a work environment that:

1. Is conducive to high quality work.

2. Values employees and encourages building of relation-ships.

3. Projects professionalism.

4. Allows us to react to program changes and growth.

5. Supports a geographically diverse workforce.

6. Allows us to safeguard investor and customer information.

7. Helps to keep our franchising program costs predictable & competitive.

8. Permits us to manage costs.

9. Is flexible and adaptive to different ways of working and the changing demographics of the workforce; individual work, team work, group work, interactions and collaborations.

10. Allows employees to feel safe and comfortable.

11. Is adaptive to new technology.

12. Uses state-of-the-art strategies for water savings, energy efficiency, materials and resources selection, and indoor environmental quality.

13. Is pleasant, inviting, and conducive to enjoying work.

Organization and culture.

Organization and culture are the most significant elements because of their impact on the workplace overall. We will discuss them further below as an integral part of creating a new emergent workplace. Our experience is that they tend to be an under represented part of workplace analysis and future thinking, probably because organization seems too obvious and unimportant at times and culture is simply hard to get to in order to identify its salient features.

Work practices, processes, patterns.

This is all about the what, why and how work is done. Many of the tools for this analysis have been well developed within the workplace planning profession over the past decade or more, including: workplace assessment surveys, participant observation, utilization studies, focus groups, social network analysis, work process mapping, etc. In varying forms, all of these tools provide useful information related to current work practices as a basis for looking at potential future practices.

There is an underlying process for all work. Processes establish the parameters for how people accomplish their work. They can be highly regularized or at times irregular. Flow is critical – what moves, how, when and where.

Tasks.

All processes are made up of discrete tasks. They can be well defined or more "ad hoc" in style. Specific tasks carry discrete needs to accomplish them – information, materials, and supports. Tasks are integrated into work processes and can be individual or group focused.

Products.

There is some type of "product" connected to every process and task. Products can be physical, but today are more typically information. They are integrated into work processes as part of the "flow". How products move is a key to effective overall work and work processes.

Support systems.

There are three big components to support systems – physical space, technology space, and human resources policies, procedures, etc. In all three areas central questions relate to: what support exists; how is it controlled; how is it assigned; what commitments are there in the future; what is envisioned in the future; and what is flexible/inflexible. A key is to identify what appears to be left out, inconsistent, or at cross purposes, and what are the trends.

Opportunities and constraints.

This is an open-ended category that is heavily dependent on judgment – both by the client and the strategist. Opportunities and constraints will naturally fall into all six of the workplace components. Looked at one way a "situation" or "characterization" will look like an opportunity and looked at from the other side, it will be a constraint. For example, a large cohort of staff about to retire is an opportunity because it opens up the organization to new thinking from a younger generation. But it is a constraint because it means there will be a large loss of well-grounded expertise and institutional memory. Finding these opportunities and constraints in all six components is important in establishing a workplace strategy that is well positioned for implementation. You leverage opportunities and work on constraints.

The emergent workplace recognizes that these key characteristics are rarely fixed; the workplace strategy needs to focus on the nature of how these characteristics are both recognized to be changing and how they could change in the future.

THE ROLE OF PROCESS

The nature of the process used to create the emergent workplace is crucial to its success. It must be open, participatory, transparent, iterative and reflective. It cannot be dependent on black box processes where "experts" go away to figure out what is the "right" solution. The creating process is, in fact, part of the emergence itself because of its impact on the participants, who are in reality the experts. Too often the planning process is considered and treated simply as a mechanism to get to a "result". In the emergent workplace the process is a goal and a result in and of itself.

The essence of process is dialog. The natural exchange that occurs in a dialog – particularly when subject to the discipline of established and structured goals - creates growth and understanding of input, direction, agreements, disagreements, opportunities and potentials with all of the participants. Simple participation is not enough because it implies that the process of creating the workplace exists independent of the people within it. Shared understandings and the growth of ideas that comes out of dialog shape the directions and details for initial implementation of an emergent workplace. By engaging in dialog about that new workplace, the participants will create important directions for new practices, patterns and behaviors. Most importantly, they will do it consciously thus enabling effective use of the new workplace and fostering continued development and change.

With a focus on dialog, there is nothing novel in a process for creating an emergent workplace. Participatory planning and design is well established as a practice, the caution is that the process should have a few basic characteristics as a foundation for good dialog. To be effective the process must be:

Open. The more open a process is, the more effective it will be. Open means that input and participation is an expectation. Open means that all information, ideas and issues are considered. At the outset it is impossible to recognize which inputs from whom are the ones that will be the most interactive and impactful in the long term. The strategic discipline aims to imagine and create a future emergent workplace. The greater the inputs, the richer the discussion that can unfold and the clearer the nature of the workplace for that particular group. An open process raises everyone's consciousness about opportunity and change. Openness also creates a sound basis to establish respect and trust within the organization and culture. Respect and trust are fundamental requirements if everyone is expected to participate fully in the creation of a new emergent workplace environment.

Relying on just one approach can lead to failure. All-hands meetings ("Town Hall" sessions) can work very well to get the word out in a highly visible way that allows leaders to stand up and answer questions and demonstrate their support for a project. Problem is that "the word" doesn't get to employees who, for whatever reason, didn't attend. Our approach is to be sure to get the same content out through multiple mechanisms orchestrated to reinforce the message, such as newsletters, internal web posts, email, staff meetings, and so on. A single channel can never be relied upon to reach 100% of the target audience.

Participatory. A participatory process structures ways for people to be included in the discovery and deliberations. It creates ways for people to participate, thereby tapping the collective imagination of the organization. The goal should be more rather than less participation. Most critically, participation feeds the dialog about opportunities and potentials that is necessary to seed the development and recognition of emergent practices, patterns and behaviors. Participation does not mean decision-making. The more people in the discussion, the better the understanding and speculation about what may emerge. Decision-making is done by the few people with that role and responsibility.

Transparent. People are naturally curious and concerned. As members of the organization, they need to know what is happening throughout the development process. Only certain people will be in position to make major decisions regarding key directions and choices for the new workplace, and everyone understands that. However, decisions need to be directly linked to, and a result of, the discovery activities in the planning process. Hard decisions and choices are an integral part of all new workplace development. It is most important that the logic for making those decisions be clear and transparent so that everyone can find a personal way to work effectively within the resulting workplace environment. Knowing how and why decisions are made is crucial for people to buy-in and progress.

Iterative. Planning is inherently future-oriented; iteration is central to effective planning. The workplace is complex. Speculating on and understanding where it is going and how it may change is equally complex. The key is to take up ideas and alternatives and test them against known practices, patterns and behaviors and against imagined scenarios and other new ideas and alternatives. It is a process that requires repeating steps, but with increasing understanding and development, and progressive refinement. You simply cannot get to a new and effective emergent workplace in a single unidirectional step. Moving quickly in a single direction assumes that you know the problem and therefore the solution – it's the traditional way to plan and design the workplace. Iteration takes a little more time up front (only a little more), but saves time in later stages because the groundwork that is laid is much more firmly developed with respect to both direction/content and everyone's understanding of where the workplace is headed and why. Iteration creates opportunities for greater and more nuanced speculations where the logic and meaning are better developed and understood. Finally, iteration provides the opportunity for organizations to internally socialize the ideas and potential changes and impacts. Complex change cannot be assimilated quickly or in big bites. It takes longer to understand and internalize the implications of change.

Reflective. Reflective is both a quality and an assumption when we talk about this kind of workplace process. The assumption is that appropriate answers need to be allowed to emerge through the dialog. The reflection is necessary because extrapolating current practices or "data" will not, by themselves, identify future practices, patterns or behaviors. The reflective quality is to be sure that potential future workplace practices, patterns and behavior are openly and consciously scrutinized and tested to see if they are in fact possible, probable, workable or applicable. Reflection simply means taking time to look carefully at where you are going and how you might get there. Avoid jumping to conclusions and then trying to prove them right after the fact.

Accountable. Transparency and participation intentionally opens the process up to being visible. This forces the process to be accountable to the participants (leaders and staff alike) and also increases the credibility of both the process and the eventual outcomes. When participants understand the nature of decisions and how they are made, though they may not agree, they tend to have higher levels of acceptance and satisfaction with the outcomes not withstanding their personal opinions. The value and opportunities in the emerging workplace continue to grow.

ORGANIZATION AND CULTURE

> *" Faced with the choice between changing one's mind and proving that there is no need to do so, almost everybody gets busy on the proof. "*
>
> John Kenneth Galbraith

Organization and culture control everything. They are the two single most important components to address and leverage in creating an emergent workplace. Focusing on organization and culture is, at its heart, a focus on the people, which is where emergence starts. The single unifying element in the workplace is the employee experience. The key is helping people be conscious about their work experience – understanding (individually and collectively) what they are doing, and why, as they do their work. This allows emergent practices, patterns and behaviors to be exposed and understood as integral to the activity of the workplace. These practices become opportunities that can be taken advantage of by individuals and groups without being dependent on changes to physical or technological settings and resources.

Physical workspace and technology tools are always designed for specific active uses. Yet we all know examples of "invented" uses (workarounds) where people have figured out how to use a space or tool for something other than that originally intended purpose. It leads to the recognition that behavior is an important variable that must be taken into account when designing workspaces and recognizes that behavior doesn't respond well to being controlled.

Hanging Neighborhood Sign at Cisco

In the course of the post-proof of concept, early roll-out of Cisco's *Cisco Connected Workplace* (CCW), we observed that groups began to hang improvised signs from the ceiling to identify a "neighborhood". In a fully unassigned environment people are free to sit anywhere. In the very open CCW environment it is easy to look around the space and see who's there; however, an early finding was that people tended to gravitate towards the same areas and naturally group with their coworkers when in the space. Taking a step towards formalizing this, groups would put up a sign to let their group know where their group usually clustered. Cisco's Workplace Resources team (the sponsors of the CCW program) quickly realized the benefit of this loose designation (being very clear to be sure that the groups themselves weren't presuming a fixed claim to the space) and agreed to provide neighborhood signs for groups that desired them in such a way as to promote a consistent branding of the space.

Herein lies the power that people bring to continuing/emergent change in the workplace. Unfortunately, getting and keeping people's attention on conscious use and exploration of workplace as an environment takes effort.

The first place to focus that effort is at the organizational level. The significant characteristic of organizations is that they can act consciously and at will – assuming there is the will. Organizations routinely choose to move in specific directions, emphasize different elements or characteristics of work, reinforce one set of behavioral patterns over another. The key is that organizations, at all levels, can take specific actions if they are seen as beneficial. The conscious opportunities within organizations need to be harnessed as part of the initial emergent workplace planning process. For best long-term effect the mechanisms used in planning should be morphed into ongoing, organizationally focused mechanisms to take advantage of succeeding emergent practices, patterns and behaviors. Specific mechanisms include:

GSA's Region 3 created a significantly strong and representative group to shepherd their mobility pilot project. Regional leadership created clear expectations and gave them "running room" to administer the pilot in the ways the group thought appropriate. The group was well balanced in terms of representing organizational groups, staff levels and individual expertise. Most critically, the group took clear and effective ownership of the pilot process, participant supports and support mechanisms, and evaluation. They turned to BPS for advice and development of some content and process features, but they retained complete control and understanding of the pilot and the opportunities and impacts it was generating for the organization.

- ***Steering/champions groups*** – The point of having a group assigned to shepherd and support change efforts is just that – you have people dedicated to and focused on change. If these groups are made up of staff level representatives, they have direct knowledge of opportunities and issues at the daily work level. They will have connection to a specific targeted part of the overall organization that they can "represent" and support throughout planning and change. As active participants, they can further the dialog that builds richness and understanding to potential workplace approaches. While it is common practice to use these groups in workplace change processes, they can have ongoing value in fostering development and communication of post-change emergent practices and behaviors. They can be particularly valuable if an organization chooses to make specific targeted changes in organization to effect a desired outcome in workplace practice or behavior.

- ***Leadership participation*** – Leaders should lead. Having those at the top out front and seen to be supportive of a new workplace provides significant impetus to development of new workplace models. Real and effective participation in creating appropriate approaches provides much more than "sign-off" support. It indicates to everyone that the organization is looking to the future and that change is valued. It helps people decide to participate themselves. Their participation is particularly valuable over the long haul if the leaders continue to support and adopt effective and visible emergent practices and behaviors.

- ***Targeted task groups*** – Task groups are a great mechanism both in planning and taking ongoing advantage of emergent practices, behavior and patterns. These focus groups are important because they are sponsored by leadership (potentially at multiple levels), they have specific tasks or concerns to address, and they are limited in duration. Their most common use is in planning. However, using them in post-implementation keeps the importance of adaptation and change front and center in an organization – a value when innovation and change is an important commodity.

Participants in a "culture group" annotating their pictoral essays of a typical day-in-the-life in their work environment.

- ***Communication mechanisms*** – Communication is a large and important category, and a significant link into organization and culture. Organizations have different preferences for what is communicated, the means, timing and audiences. Some organizations communicate with great effectiveness and grace, while others stumble badly. The emerging popularity of social media is no less than completely redefining communication, and will continue to evolve at an accelerating rate in the foreseeable future. At the very least, technology, writ large, is impacting organizations and culture, enabling increasing degrees of mobility and challenging the prevalence of "face-to-face" cultures and communication practices. Effective communication is no longer inextricably linked with place, but is still central to organizational effectiveness and cultural development.

We have found that with some focused attention, people can identify key social and cultural characteristics of their immediate and larger organizations. It can be a significant help in creating an appropriate strategy.

Now we get to politics, power and influence. These are the inevitable, important but often unsightly parts of organizations. The key is to recognize the significance of politics, power and influence because they will affect the flow and direction of change overall and the potential for emergent practices to germinate and develop. There are no clever answers or mechanisms to address them since they are more context than mechanism. Awareness is central to effectively tapping them in opportunistic ways.

Culture is the most powerful force, but everyone says it is slow to change. Our experience is that is true, especially for many deeply embedded characteristics. However, it's not true across the board. There are culturally defined behaviors that are more adaptable and quickly responsive to changing forces. Culture is an attribute of communities. Communities / organizations, insofar as they are comprised of, and defined by, the membership of individuals, share common interests, beliefs, values, purpose, etc., i.e. culture (see Figure 2. Individual-Organizational Affinity, above). While individuals might adapt their personal views or practices in response to community relatively rapidly, the reverse happens at a slower pace due to the relative strength of influence as relates to culture. The desire by an individual to conform to a group culture is more prevalent than the rare charismatic leader's personal influence over a community.

Attunement and attachment are central to understanding local culture. Attunement is what people pay attention to. What people pay attention to reflects cultural values and priorities - key aspects of culture. "Attachment" reflects the degree to which a community or organization permits investment of attributed value or meaning to a particular asset or characteristic of the community. This can be a measure of resistance to change. We observe, time and again, people in organizations clinging to old, tired (sometimes derelict) workspaces because they are comfortable in their environment. Think about this in terms of your favorite pair of shoes – you like them because they're comfortable. When you slip them on, memories of past experiences while wearing your favorite shoes flood your subconscious. You feel good. When confronted by someone suggesting or insisting that it's time to replace the old shoes, you quickly mount a rigorous defense of the value of keeping the shoes. Attachment is strongly emotional, but usually less rational. In the case of the familiarity of the old workspace, we've seen just this kind of response, despite all rational arguments in favor of updating the space.

At the US Agency for International Development (USAID) – as we find with many organizations – even though employees are working in a very old, tired work environment, they display an "interesting" attitude toward the prospect of changing to something new. The early and clear preference expressed by a vocal minority is for the project team to go away and leave them alone. They want to avoid the disruption that is inevitable with any renovation project. People argued that (despite their space being eighteen years old, dark, dingy, etc.) it would be a better use of taxpayer dollars to keep the current space and spend the money on programs. We determined that the biggest hangup was actually difficulty with the abstract notion of the design of the new space, and the fears associated with the intangible unknowns represented by the architect's drawings combined with strong skepticism that the Agency would actually follow through with the project. The post occupancy evaluation found that the space is generally very successful, with people's fears having been allayed.

Before   After

Attachment is one thing. Attunement applies less as an emotional bias, but more as a practical awareness by individuals and the group. What attracts the attention of the group depends on what the group defines as its purpose and mission, as reflected in the goals, priorities and the work undertaken. Leadership plays a central role here. What the group is attuned to distinguishes its ordinary state; by contrast, anything that falls outside this normal focus can be seen as a threat to the current state, or status quo.

> *"The difficulty lies not so much in developing new ideas as in escaping from old ones."*
>
> John Maynard Keynes

What's important to an organization, and what are people holding on to or reluctant to give up? To what degree is an organization open to new ideas? Attunement and attachment can be used as approaches for illuminating how organizations understand certain behaviors that are naturally part of the social nature of work - sharing, interrupting, interaction time frames, the need to concentrate on individual tasks, etc.

This relates to the emergent workplace in important ways. The workplace itself has become accepted as having an impact on attraction and retention of employees *vis-à-vis* the organization. Each of the principal characteristics of the workplace (depicted in Figure 1., p. 3) contributes to this as – importantly – experienced by the employee (at the center of the diagram). While culture is depicted separately (often thought of for its "softer", or less quantifiable qualities than the other workplace characteristics), it could

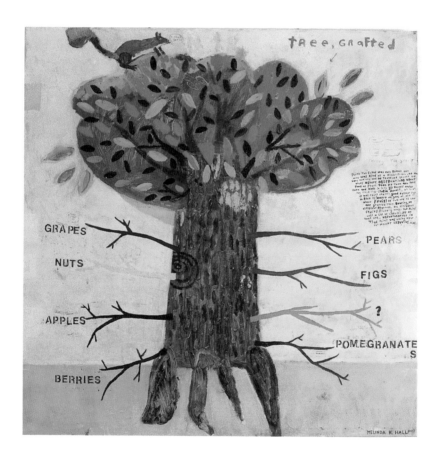

CHAPTER FOUR

Describing the Emergent Workplace

So, after all this, what does the emergent workplace "look like"? On one hand, the answer is relatively easy because there are a few basic characteristics of the physical and technology workspaces that seem to support emergent behaviors and practices. On the other hand, you have to look deeper to identify particular support systems that effectively open opportunities for people and the organization to grow. In this chapter we will describe what we have found to be the key elements in the physical, technological and support system spaces that allow emergence to thrive.

PHYSICAL WORKSPACE

Physical workspace is central to the emergent workplace dilemma – you have to make commitments and investments well ahead of the time future practices, patterns and behaviors have developed. Unlike traditional programming and design, emergent workplace design has to be done based on assumptions that inevitably will change. If you can't reliably identify knowable and specific needs, the focus should be on creating a basic structure or framework of space that is amenable to new and different work and behavioral traits. The key question is how do you craft such a framework to be adaptable to ongoing contributions from emergent practices, patterns and behaviors? The question is easy but the answer is much more complex due to the multiple variables affecting the workplace. Let's first look at ways to understand and potentially simplify those variables.

The first and most important variable is not physical space itself. It's the people. Understanding how a particular group of people behave, interact and use their workspace provides significant clues to what a framework of settings can do for them in the future. This goes back again to the organization and culture, but this time focused on individuals in the workspace. The more you can understand about the people and how they work and interact, the easier it is discover how they use space and where new emergent practices, patterns and behaviors may develop. It is important to understand how the workspace can provide a framework for these individual, and subsequently, group behaviors.

The second and third variables are based on the type of work people are engaged in – either working by oneself or working with others. It is the nature and patterns of those two, maybe not-so-simple, activities that add complexity to the workplace environment, and that makes it susceptible to emergence. One might guess that it is the working together that sees greater impact from emergence. True, but not completely, because today's technologies have provided significant resources and tools for people to modify how and where they do their individual heads-down work. In addition, while the typology is simple, the variations in workspace today – both available and needed/desired – are voluminous. The variations and the words used to describe them are sometimes so subtle as to make distinctions difficult for all but the designers.

In the next section we will describe important characteristics of these three variables that should form the basis for creating an effective framework of settings and resources.

WORKSPACE FRAMEWORK CHARACTERISTICS

People Characteristics:

- *Change response* – How do people and the organization respond to change, especially changes "from the outside"? We generally find it is based on the employee experience, reflecting individual and group attitudes. Response to change is an important indicator of how people will adapt to and create new patterns and behaviors within a new workplace environment/framework.

- *Interactivity characteristics/needs* – Much has been made recently about differences in individual needs, e.g. extroverts and introverts. These differences do make a difference and finally there are ways to accommodate the differences in the workspace. Interaction isn't unidimensional, but encompassing multiple modes, such as face-to-face, by telephone, one-to-one, one-to-many, via email or SMS, Twitter or other instant messaging interface technologies including social media, and so on.

- *Information flow* – What role do the individuals play in the flow of information across the workplace? What is the impact of time on decision-making? How do people deal with complexity in the work?

- *Cultural idiosyncrasies* – What is particular about the local culture that influences its member's interaction with the environment? For instance: how and where do they socialize – if at all; what are the "rules" of workplace behavior; what are expectations related to communications, etc.?

Individual Work Characteristics

- *Frequency and duration* – Patterns of work matter a lot in creating appropriate frameworks. Some work is done in "20 second sound bites" while other work requires long periods of focused uninterrupted time. These patterns tend to be task specific and less responsive to emergent changes.

- *Severability* – Is work place-dependent? Individual work is sometimes managed or supervised with an emphasis on "showing up" and "by the clock": this kind of approach relies on being located centrally, with a high reliance on physical presence (not necessarily related to work output). In the case of knowledge work, the work itself can sometimes be recognized as severable from the workspace – i.e. not dependent on being performed in any particular place. This kind of work is often best managed by evaluating the actual outcomes or work product as opposed to tracking logistical details of the time and place where the work was actually performed.

- *Interruptibility* – What impacts are there from interruptions? Depending on the nature of the work, interruptions can pose a real threat to productivity. For example, tasks involving deep concentration, such as reading and writing, can be difficult to perform in instances where the work environment fails to provide adequate visual and acoustic separation from high activity areas adjacent to where people are trying to concentrate. By contrast, other kinds of work benefit greatly from deliberate measures to promote interactivity and collaboration. Design work and other innovation-seeking work benefit from lively, messy spaces where people are highly prone to interruptions.

- *Specific needs* – Some work depends on ready access to certain resources (e.g. central records, secure restricted-access networks, specialty equipment, etc.), which may represent specific parameters that could determine particular aspects of the work. The key for establishing specific needs is to distinguish between current needs/practices and those that may occur in the future. In today's work environment, the biggest trend leading to different future support needs is the transition from wet to digital signatures. What else might apply in the future?

- *Performance* – What are the key characteristics of performance across the range of individual and group activities and business requirements? These performance characteristics will help define some of the other categories described here for both individual and group activities.

- Summary: Take care when describing individual work because over-generalizations can apply too loosely, becoming relatively useless as a basis for creating an effective framework.

Group Work

- *Interactive qualities* – If it's group work, it means people are interacting. The first question is: what are the modes, mechanisms and locational/timing relationships? Some work is more active and loud while other work is interactive yet passive and quiet. Are there characteristic patterns driven by the nature of the work or the culture of the organization? What characteristics of the interactions might flow through and into newly emergent behaviors and practices? How do the interactive qualities vary across an organization and potential job/task types?

- *Frequency and duration* – The how often and how long of interactions can vary significantly across groups and time. Consistent patterns over time have the potential to continue to be stable in the future particularly if they are directly tied to consistent underlying business needs and processes. Significant variation in either frequency or duration simply means that a workspace framework needs to provide a greater array of supportive elements. Short over-the-computer interactions need a different workspace than long-planned-in-advance meetings, even if they are of the same small size.

- *Size variation* – Meetings can vary from the small two-person computer-sharing session to a very large session. Meeting size can also vary over time, either in regular or irregular patterns. As with other characteristics, consistency over time can be an important influence if the underlying factors are seen to be fundamental to the business in the future. Today size can vary dramatically in terms of people attending in person versus people attending interactions remotely. Remote linkages are as much a part of small group interactions as for large group ones. The supports differ considerably by size. We find that small group interactions are more susceptible to and impacted by immediate and quick emergent practices.

- *Distribution* – Distributed organizations often include members resident in different time zones and countries who still need to work together. How can the workplace bridge some of these gaps (time, distance and "intangible" qualities)?

What does all this mean for creating that workspace framework? Remember, everyone has to sit somewhere. The issue is providing appropriate places for people to work (sitting or standing, alone or together) that support flexibility and adaptability. Providing sets of alternative resources to choose from that accommodate the various needs gives people and groups important choice and control over their immediate work setting. If not useful at the time, users can choose to ignore them. Over time, this may lead to to re-purposing. This is what we refer to as a framework of workspace resources: resources designed for choice and adaptability rather than designed for and assigned to specific uses and users. Our experience shows that more workspace choice and tools to choose and effectively make use of those choices is a net benefit to all organizations.

Cisco Connected Workplace (CCW)

Cisco didn't rush into or stumble upon their CCW program. The early efforts of their Workplace Effectiveness team drew on even earlier experience from supporting their rapid field sales office expansion through the mid and late 1990's. The focus of the CCW model is to de-couple "butts-in-seats" from the workplace planning process by integrating their own technology solutions through what is referred to as their "Cisco on Cisco" program.

The physical workplace provides a wide range of alternate workspace settings for employees to choose from, including quiet rooms for individual use, audio privacy rooms for small groups and teams to use when they want to avoid disrupting colleagues doing individual work, casual seating, break areas, touchdowns, and a variety of desk types - all designed to enable work to flow in the manner which best suits the employees.

Today, Cisco employees worldwide share in one of the most robust technology space environments available, including gigabit speed WLAN throughout the workspace, mesh-network WiFi access on corporate campuses, WebEx Connected PC VPN access, WebEx Social interface for online communities, Telepresence, document sharing, instant messaging, presence status, and more.

Key to making CCW a highly effective approach for Cisco is that it is equally embraced by employees and their managers. The combination of the physical and technology spaces, along with clear understanding and support of employees working anywhere they need to be, are some of the essential ingredients to their success.

TECHNOLOGY WORKSPACE

Technology is central to work today and the most significant driver of emergent practices, patterns and behaviors. Data has finally become digital in large part and the rapid expansion of mobile technologies has freed people up from the limitations of "having to sit at their desk". Technology has now become its own workspace, making its presence felt every bit as much as the physical workspace. The technology dilemma is opposite that of physical space – it moves too fast and is occasionally disruptive. Organizations struggle to adapt at the speed at which new opportunities or demands are created in the technology space. Budgets and investments in previous systems limit formal organizational response – at least at the whole organization level. However, technology is easy for individuals to invest in and experiment with in their work. The BYOD (bring your own device) approach is simply a recognition that there are plenty of early adopters and pioneers making demands on the technology workspace.

So what to pay attention to in creating an emergent workplace? Unfortunately, you can't pin it down (because it's constantly emerging!) particularly with respect to the specific technologies. However, we do know from observation that there are a few key

---

Sometimes new tools and the access they bring can generate interesting new work approaches, even at a small scale. As part of GSA's pilot they handed out iPads to the participants who had changed to fully mobile work. The uses people developed were quite varied and creative. In one case a designer put all her client plans on the device to have access in the field. When the interaction with the client required new thinking, she simply put some tracing paper over the iPad and worked out a new design. It's a small emergent practice that could lead to new ways and flexibility of interacting with her clients.

---

characteristics that create a technology space amenable to emergent use.

Electronic data. Not all data is yet electronic and maybe some small parts of it will never be. However, the incredible array of information available through electronic form is the central catalyst of emergent practices, behaviors and patterns in the workplace. As the transition continues, its influence will become even greater.

Immediate access. People want, and in some cases need, immediate access to information and each other. There are multiple ways of getting there today and we assume that there will be even more entries in the future. Immediate also implies seamless. I don't want to have to switch access methods or re-boot or change devices as I move from place to place and program to program. Smooth and immediate access is the key.

Multi-channeled. Each channel type delivers different and distinct benefits. This is a place where choice has clear benefit. More choices provide more opportunity to create new and better ways of working. Variation generates the capacity to establish new and more effective relationships and work practices and patterns in all organizations, particularly ones that are distributed.

Accessibility, flexibility and redundancy. These are all characteristics of a robust technology space. They describe characteristics of the hardware, software and the network itself. People need and want timely access to information and other people. Flexibility in how they get that access and how they work with the tools and information to which they have access enables people to work more on their own terms. Continuous or persistent access means that if one channel/technology is down there are alternative ways of getting work done, which improves productivity. Specifics will vary by organization and certainly over time, but the criteria hold.

SUPPORT SYSTEMS

All workplaces are supported by underlying systems that provide resources, guidance and control. Some are obvious like security, maintenance, physical facilities and technology. Others might be less obvious, such as human resources for policies, training and counseling. The key to all these support systems in facilitating an emergent workplace is that less works better than more – as in control. With freedom comes responsibility. Conventional workplaces may be reliant on central management controls, such as centralized corporate real estate and facilities, IT or HR organizations. Such centralized controls (e.g. reservation systems or strict limits on personnel movement) may stifle the freedom of local user spontaneity. At the same time, decentralizing such controls may be an unanticipated burden on organizations accustomed to having internal support systems at their beck and call.

Appropriate balance is the key with these support systems. Control should only be established and applied when needed for some clear and intended reason. For example, the traditional workplace cared where everyone was at any point in time – where would they sit (space assignments, IT tracking, mail delivery, etc.), when would they be there (office hours, limits on off-site work, etc.). The key with emergent workplace support systems is that they be as open and flexible as possible to allow for new and potentially more effective practices and behaviors. Supports also need to be accessible and *used* by employees to be effective. For example, with nearly every one of our clients, we find that managers are the stake-holders under the most pressure to change from the traditional workplace to the emergent workplace. Most managers are vested with the responsibility to see that the work gets done. While many managers focus on outcomes and less on what it takes to produce the desired results, some managers apply more of a control methodology to making sure that each of their employees is showing up and "present" at work as the indication that work is getting done. Support systems, such as telework programs and related policies, often stress the importance of training and communication; however, such supports remain ineffective when they aren't taken advantage of.

CHAPTER FIVE

The Emergent Workplace Today

O ur experience and observation is that the emergent workplace is coming as a practice. Because the process of getting to an emergent workplace is different from current practice in its fundamental assumptions and participatory requirements, today we see it only in small bits and pieces. It takes two important resources to get to an effective emergent workplace. The first is a client – organization or business – that recognizes the value of change and will invest the time and money to get there over the long haul. That investment means individual and organizational commitment of time and flexibility. The second is a set of consultants – planners, designers, change managers – who recognize the fluidity of the emergence process and have the tools and skills to work with unpredictability. The emergent workplace falls squarely into the category of "wicked problems"[1] where tradi-

---

1   Rittel, Horst; "On the Planning Crisis: Systems Analysis of the 'First and Second Generations'; University of California, Berkeley.

tional planning and design approaches are inadequate because they cannot effectively deal with the fluid, complex, and highly political nature of emergent change. Practitioners need to be able to deal with these characteristics and still find solutions for an emergent workplace.

WORKPLACES NOT WORKSPACES

The focus in the emergent workplace is on the workplace, not the workspace. No matter which workplace model you use, the workspace is just one component of a working environment. The glue in all these models is the people. It is employees that bring context and meaning to all aspects of work and the workplace. We always need to address all six workplace components (in the BPS model) to effectively create and support an emergent workplace. Central to that effort must be a focus on and inclusion of employees to create appropriate and ongoing meaning and understanding of available opportunities.

Attitude matters. Attitude is the most reliable predictor of future - i.e. emergent - behavior. A plethora of academic studies, including a seminal 1977 analysis by Ajzen and Fischbein[2] document the veracity of this claim. We hold this as an important truth concerning the employee experience in the workplace. Debates rage on about mobility, telework, "virtual work", and so on. All the debates tend to focus on worker productivity (leaving quality of the work as an implicit assumption). Our particular bias is that the worker – and the employee experience - represents the most

---

2   Ajzen, I., & Fishbein, M. (1977). Attitude-behavior relations: A theoretical analysis and review of empirical research. Psychological Bulletin, 84, 888-918.

important aspect of the debate. Arguably, if we can focus on the employee experience, and their attitudes about the workplace, the prediction is that individual and organizational, and therefore business, results will reflect that experience.

Attitude also matters in the spread and adoption of potential emergent work practices and behaviors. Research on habitual behavior is important to the emergent workplace - because emergence is also about breaking old habits and establishing new ones. We know that old habits create strong resistance to change because habits are efficient. They help us get our work done. We also know that new habits take careful attention because old habits do not actually go away, they just stop being used.

SUSTAINING THE EMERGENT WORKPLACE

We are frequently asked how change can be sustained. The answer is both easy and difficult at the same time. Change is easy to sustain as the organization, culture and individuals become comfortable with it as an ongoing practice. Some organizations are naturally inclined to accept and even welcome change and individual input to change. These organizations have little difficulty in creating/adapting to an emergent workplace. The other organizations need to spend time and energy focusing on change and its benefits. It requires directed action as described above to create an organizational/cultural environment accepting of ongoing change. This takes time and energy. Our experience is that it is difficult for many organizations to maintain a concerted level of effort or commit to the types of policy and management changes that are required to integrate and maintain beneficial emergent change. It is all too easy to fall back into the lower energy levels of old organizational and cultural habits. Benefits of change are seen differently by different organizations, and they tend to act on what they can see.

WHY IT'S WORTH THE EFFORT

A big part of the value of the emergent workplace lies in two connected characteristics: it is both adaptable and malleable. Because change is fundamental to an emergent culture and organization, new opportunities, tools or impacts are easily and naturally integrated into day-to-day work practices, behaviors and patterns. The organization and its work is naturally adaptable in an effort to be efficient and effective as a business. Organizations vary in their level of adaptability in the six workplace components, with physical and technology space typically being the least adaptable. However, the greater the organizational comfort with embedded change, the greater the use of emergent workplace opportunities.

Cisco took several years to build their CCW program, testing the approach across a variety of business units and geographies and consciously tweaking the approach to ensure maximum flexibility and sustainability. The supply chain manager said it well, as previously noted, when he proclaimed, "it is paying for itself more than you know right now."

Because the emergent workplace is naturally adaptable, it is also malleable. Malleable simply means that it is easier to undertake initiatives to drive intentional change. Businesses often need to change direction, modify processes, add product/services, or simply change organizational structure. They are all intentional changes that are made easier when the organization is naturally adaptable.

Perhaps, most importantly, our experience is that the emergent workplace tends to be more vibrant and dynamic. It's more transparent and supportive of interaction; people interact more, even if it is at a distance. There is more energy. The emergent workplace takes more focus and work at its inception, but it pays that energy back over the long term.

CHAPTER SIX

The Emergent Workplace Tomorrow

What is the emergent workplace of tomorrow? We actually don't know...at least not in detail. It's the problem with emergence - you can't know until it appears. By default, we tend to stick to what we know. It feels somehow safer than venturing down the future path towards the unknown. It's easier to imagine and convince others of the downside of a new approach, though this choice carries its own set of risks.

> *"We selectively hear only what we recognize, interpret*
> *what we hear based on our past views and feelings, and*
> *draw conclusions much like those we have drawn before.*
> *... actions tend to preserve the status quo, even though the*
> *actors may sincerely espouse an intention to change. "[1]*

Otto Scharmer

1　Scharmer, C. Otto (2009-01-01). Theory U: Learning from the Future as It Emerges (Kindle Locations 111-114). Berrett-Koehler Publishers. Kindle Edition.

Nevertheless, we do know something about that future workplace. It is, and will continue to be, shaped by the community of people who work there. Just as the context for each organization is different, so the workplace context should be attuned to the organization it houses. Some organizations are just more free-wheeling than others. What sort of workplace is successful for one might be disastrous for another. What's important is to understand the nature and the vision of the organization and proceed from there into the murky, or bright, future.

All organizations, and thereby their workplaces, will undergo change sooner or later. The timing is up to the leadership and stakeholders. Pursuing change requires overcoming inherent, omnipresent biases. Process is key; in other words, the extent to which the prospective future is made relevant to the stakeholders, the greater the likelihood there will be buy-in and successful implementation. Attitude toward change can make the transitions easier or harder; attitude, however, cannot forestall the inevitable.

Just as an appropriate process can contribute to making change a viable possibility, the emergent workplace itself is a framework that creates and promotes opportunity. Our environment shapes us. The workplace, in the complex system of all its component parts, is the environment that shapes the future of the organization. Successful workplaces respond to, as well as influence the organizations they are created for. Openness to the future and what is possible – as a cultural mindset – can be reflected in the character of the workplace and thereby orient the organization forward. This dialectic is at the heart of the emergent workplace.

The emergent workplace is difficult for all of us to imagine. After all, abstractions of work must necessarily be generalized, and will inevitably not account for significant but hidden details and relationships. Our future is only limited by our imagination. Imagining the emergent workplace requires the willingness to disregard the status quo and embrace uncertainty. It takes a bit of time and can, at times, be a bit rocky. But the results can be both instrumental and energizing for the organization and its people.

What's the future at Cisco and GSA's Region 3? At Cisco the CCW workplace approach is already fully embedded in over two million square feet at the headquarters and many other sites. The company recently announced its commitment to continue to roll out CCW campus-wide, given it's proven effectiveness in supporting current work and developing work practices.

GSA Region 3 is in the process of moving to a new physical location. In preparation, the Public Building Service is transitioning to a fully mobile work environment. We expect the number and significance of emergent practices will continue to grow as the change happens.

We believe that both organizations are well positioned to support a robust emergent workplace that will put them in good stead in the future.

Glossary

assigned	Agreement that an individual (cubicle or enclosed office) seating or group (team room, war room, conference room) setting is reserved for the use by a named individual or group.
brand	The experience (positive or negative) of the consumer (client, customer) of offered products and services.
collaborate	To work jointly with others or together especially in an intellectual endeavor.
change management	We refer to change management in this book in the context of workplace change. It's an approach to helping people with the transition to a new workplace so that they can continue to be effective in their work.
the "Cloud"	Jargon, fast becoming a formal term referring to the inter-connected network space – or platform – including the Internet, VPN's, VoIP telephony, web-conferencing, websites, remote servers and storage, software-as-service, etc., and all the devices they conect, enabling diffused, distributed computing and data processing across the platform, i.e. cloud computing.
emergence	From Wikipedia: "Emergence is the way complex systems and patterns arise out of a multiplicity of relatively simple interactions."

emergent workplace	The emergent workplace is one that specifically fosters the development and adoption of emergent behaviors, practices and work patterns. It is much more open, flexible, and diverse in creating choices than traditional workplaces.
hoteling	Arrangement whereby mobile workers or visitors can use unassigned workstations in a subject work space. Like hotel rooms, sometimes hoteling workstations can be reserved in advance by means of a reservation system. "Free addressing" and "touchdown" workstations are terms often used in a similar sense.
innovation	"To introduce as or as if new ... to make changes: do something in a new way" (Webster's Collegiate Dictionary); process of developing an unproven concept or idea into a viable product or service. Innovation process: idea generation; idea development; commercialization / implementation.
mobile worker	An individual who has the option or need to perform work from a variety of locations, who may or may not be assigned an individual workstation.
mobility	Ability to work from any location; supported by policy, technology infrastructure and tools, and physical settings which promote the ability to choose the best place to accomplish the work at hand. An integrated workplace strategy that enables and supports employees working from anywhere best suited for them to accomplish the work they and their organizations need done, including tactical approaches to working from chosen locations such as telework, "hot-desking" (use of shared, touch-down workstations), team rooms, huddle rooms, wireless network access, shared / unassigned workstations, and so on.
neighborhood	Area which is assigned to a particular group within an open work area without assigned seating.
physical workspace	Physical workspace is all of the places we need to use to do our work – desks, meeting rooms, specialty rooms, etc. In today's workplace, those physical resources do not have to be in centralized locations – the office.

pilot	Experimental project of defined / limited scope with specific objectives to test assumptions and aspects of the design (e.g. features, behaviors, other performance measures). Assumption in pilot projects is that some aspects of the design will be demonstrated to be successful and other aspects unsuccessful. Sometimes referred to as "proof of concept." Pilot projects may or may not become operational models for deployment or implementation depending on agreed upon success.
precinct boundary	distinct space demarkations between adjacent organizations collocated in a common space, often used for accounting purposes for operating expenses tied to assigned space occupied by an organization.
shared use spaces	Settings for individual or group activities which by agreement and in practice are available for use on a shared basis as determined by the business group "owner" of the space. Successful sharing of space is often enabled by adopting use guidelines and "etiquette" to ensure maximum benefit is realized by the organization.
social network analysis	The methodical analysis of networks of social relationships. Within the workplace it is used to identify significant relationships to inform development of new organizational structures and key features and arrangements of space in a new work environment.
technology workspace	Technology today establishes a digital space that is central to work – i.e. the technology workspace. It is distinguished from physical workspace in that with proper linkages and tools it is useable from any location.
Telepresence	Video conferencing system, usually high-definition video and audio, often including close to lifesize screen images of participants. Telepresence systems can often link multiple sites in a single session.
telework	Work from home. Telework often involves a formalized telework agreement in which the employee and supervisor set forth specific expectations regarding performance, schedule, communications, accountability and so on.

traditional work-place	The "traditional workplace" focuses on workspace over other environmental elements (e.g. policies, technology, etc.). Workspaces are typically assigned to an individual or group and are generally assumed to support most of the daily work/task needs of that individual.
utilization	Frequency and duration of use as determined by physical presence in a particular work space. Measured by direct observation of persons using individual or group settings.
virtual	Concept of working together regardless of location – generally connotes work contribution across multiple locations shared among a distributed team.
VPN	Virtual Private Network. Extends a private, secure network across a public network, such as the Internet.
work space	The physical place where work occurs, comprised of settings that support individual work and work in groups
workplace	The context of work; various factors that make up the work environment including culture, work process, support systems (e.g. technology infrastructure and tools), organization structure, physical environment and organizational policies.
WLAN	Wireless local area network - technology allowing computing devices to wirelessly connect to a local area network. Increasingly referred to as WiFi, especially when the local area network includes Internet access.

Acknowledgements

"Great persons are able to do great kindnesses."

Don Quixote (Cervantes)

Thank yous are due to some particular folks for their encouragement and support as we undertook this effort.

Judi Heerwagen, Gervais Tompkin and Don Doyle, with each of whom we've enjoyed numerous opportunities to collaborate over many years, have all generously taken time to not only read through manuscripts but also have imparted much wisdom through their comments and suggestions. We can't thank you enough!

Many thanks to June Langhoff, our copy editor, for keeping us focused and on point.

Dan Jansenson deserves our thanks as well, and credit for encouraging us onward towards commiting our thoughts to these pages. It was Dan who shared his positive experience with self-publishing and prompted us down this path. He also provided us with very thoughtful feedback on the book design that has helped us make this a better book.

Melinda Hall has a truly warm way of delightfully expressing her curiosity for the world through her paintings, some of which she has most generously and graciously shared, as we've exhibited in this book. We are grateful. To see more of her wonderful work visit:

http://www.melinda-k-hall.com.

Made in the USA
Charleston, SC
18 September 2013